TWINS

Read aloud the sounds on each line.

Two sounds on each line are the same. Put a box around each of them.

SOUND OFF

Circle the sound each Hebrew letter makes.

Say the sound and the name of the Hebrew letter.

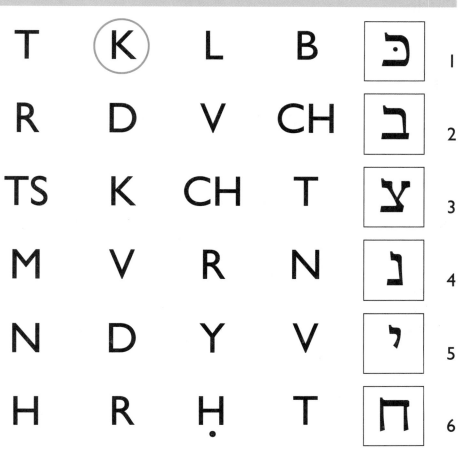

ל ‏ ו ‏ ו ‏ ו ‏ ו ‏ ו ‏ ו

COLOR THE SOUNDS

Read aloud the two Hebrew sounds in each balloon. Color the balloon if the two sounds are the same.

How many balloons did you color? _____

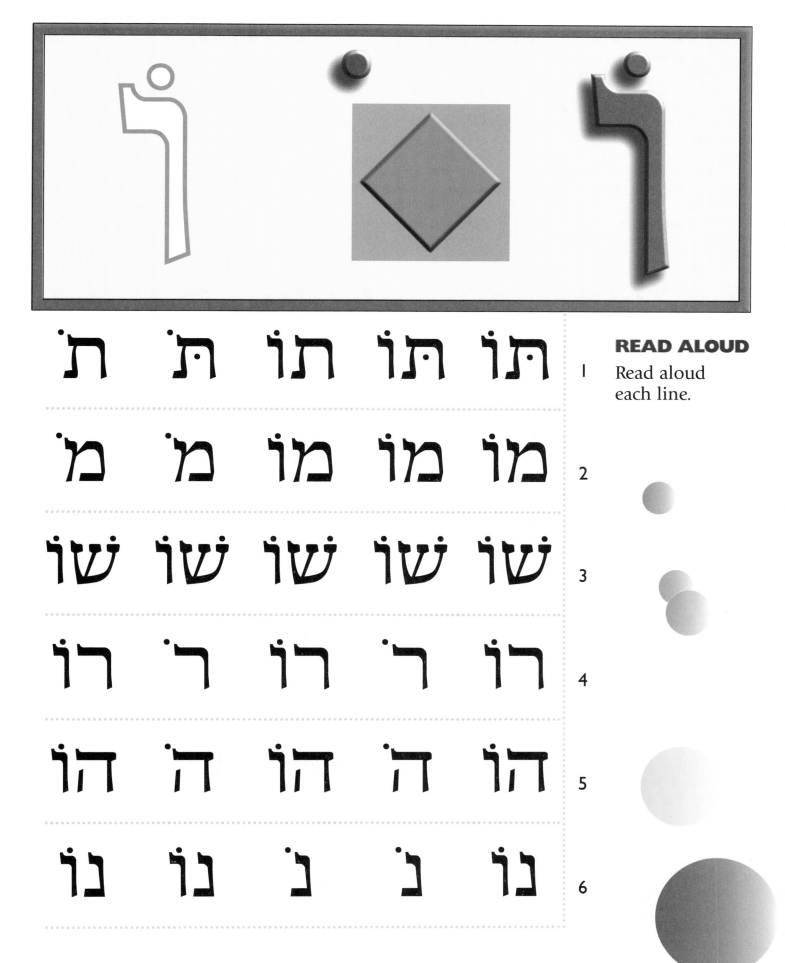

READ ALOUD

Read aloud
each line.

1   תָּ   תֹּ   תּוֹ   תֹּ   תּוֹ

2   מָ   מֹ   מוֹ   מֹ   מוֹ

3   שׁוֹ   שׁוֹ   שׁוֹ   שׁוֹ   שׁוֹ

4   רוֹ   רֹ   רוֹ   רֹ   רוֹ

5   הוֹ   הֹ   הוֹ   הֹ   הוֹ

6   נוֹ   נֹ   נוֹ   נֹ   נוֹ

Read aloud the sounds on each line.

One sound on each line is different. Circle it.

How many times do you see a letter and vowel that together make the sound "oh"?

_____

אֹו	אֹו	אֶ	אֹ	אֹ	1
דָּ	דֹו	דֹ	דֹו	דֹו	2
כֹּו	כָ	כֹו	כֹ	כֹ	3
בֹ	בֹו	בָ	בֹ	בֹ	4
חֹ	חֹו	חֹ	חֹ	חָ	5
עֹו	עֹו	עֹ	עָ	עֹ	6
לֹ	יֹן	יֹן	יֹן	יָ	7
לָ	לֹ	לֹו	לֹ	לֹו	8
קֹו	קָ	קֹו	קֹ	קֹ	9

63

RINGS

Play Rings with a friend. With your eyes shut, take turns aiming your pencil at the circled sounds on the page. Read the Hebrew sound closest to where your pencil lands. Add the number in the ring to your score. Who has the highest score after five turns?

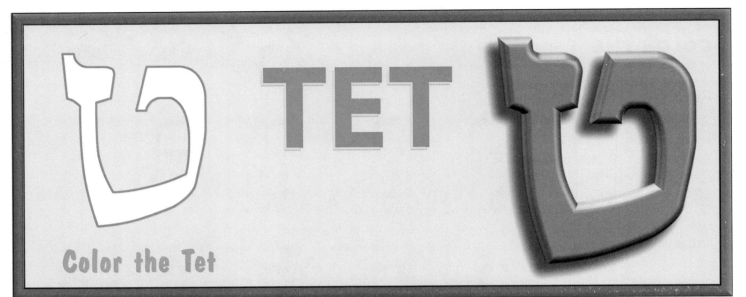

Color the Tet

SEARCH AND CIRCLE

Read aloud the sound each letter makes.

One letter on each line makes a different sound. Circle it.

טַלִּית

ט ט ט ט ט (ה) 1

ט ט צ ט ט ט 2

ט ט ט ט מ 3

ט ט כ ט ט 4

ט ט ט ל ט 5

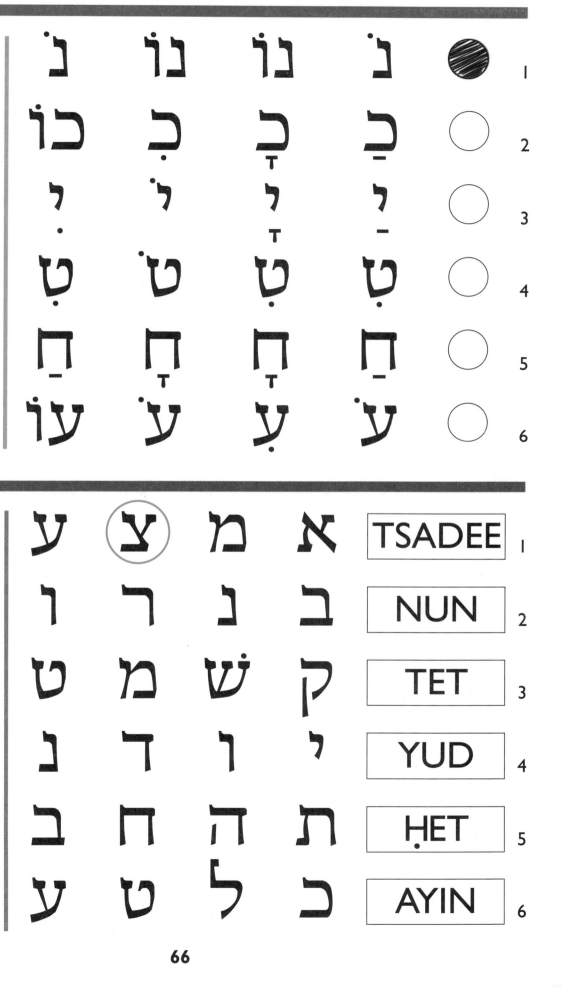

COLOR THE CIRCLE

Read aloud the sounds on each line.

Color the circle if all the sounds on the line are the same.

NAME THE LETTER

Circle the Hebrew letter named in the box.

TSADEE	1
NUN	2
TET	3
YUD	4
ḤET	5
AYIN	6

66

TRACE THE LETTER

ט ט ט ט ט ט ט ט

PATHWAYS

Find the path that leads each letter to its matching picture.

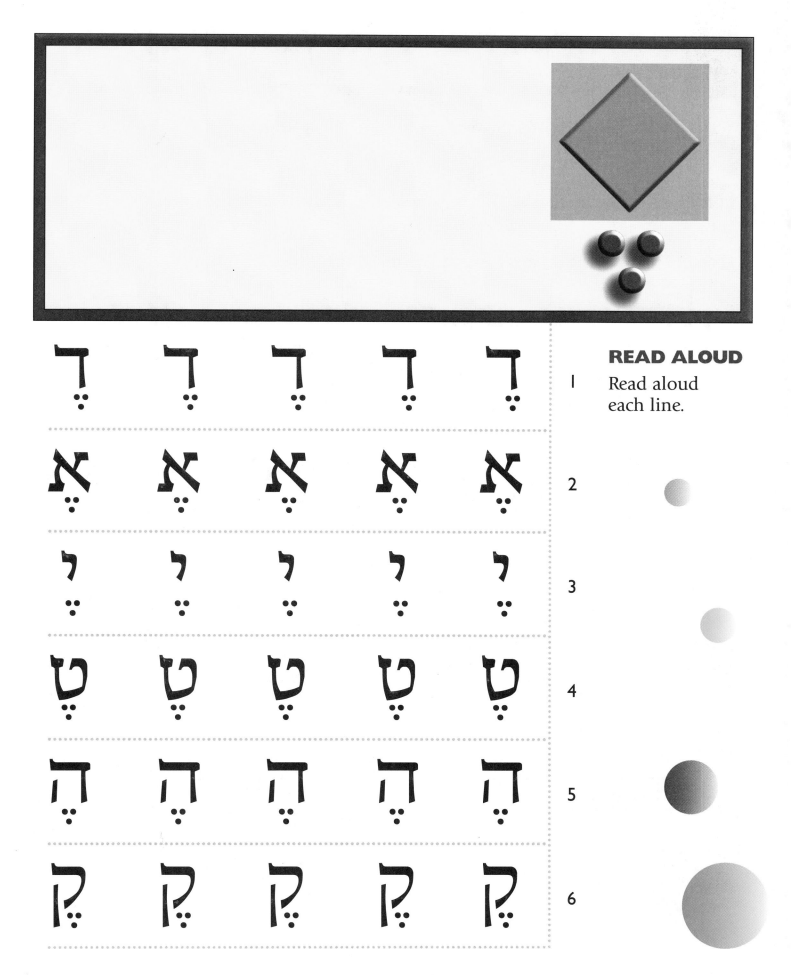

1 Read aloud
   each line.

דֶּ דֶּ דֶּ דֶּ דֶּ

אֶ אֶ אֶ אֶ אֶ 2

לֶ לֶ לֶ לֶ לֶ 3

טֶ טֶ טֶ טֶ טֶ 4

הֶ הֶ הֶ הֶ הֶ 5

קֶ קֶ קֶ קֶ קֶ 6

SEARCH AND CIRCLE

Read aloud the sounds on each line.

One sound on each line is different. Circle it.

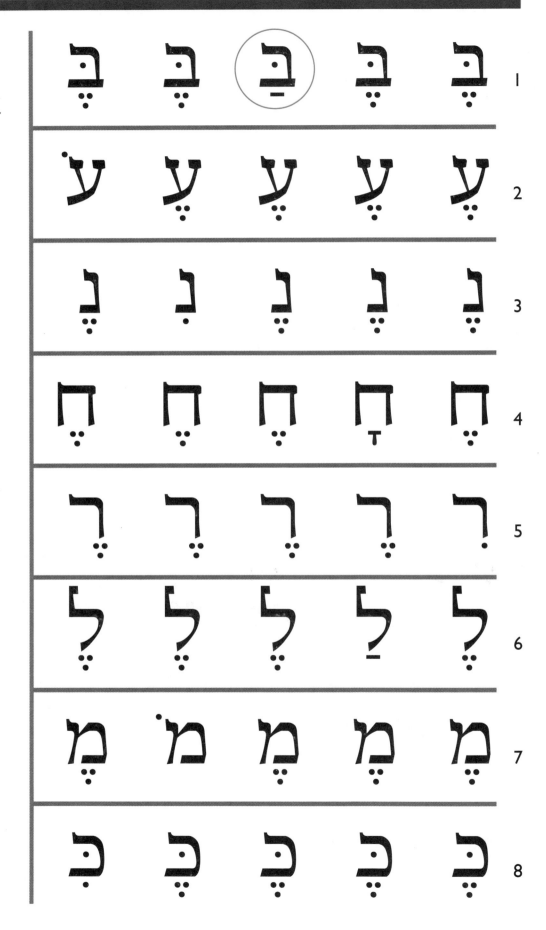

בֵּ   בֵּ   (בַ)   בֵּ   בֵּ   1

עֱ   עֱ   עֱ   עֱ   עֱ   2

נֵ   נֵ   נִ   נֵ   נֵ   3

חֵ   חֵ   חֵ   חָ   חֵ   4

רֵ   רֵ   רֵ   רֵ   רִ   5

לֵ   לֵ   לֵ   לַ   לֵ   6

מֵ   מִ   מֵ   מֵ   מֵ   7

כִ   כֵ   כֵ   כֵ   כֵ   8

Color the Pay

PAY

פ פ פ תּ פ | 1

פ פ כ פ פ | 2

פ פ פ פ בּ | 3

פ פ פ שׁ פּ | 4

פ פ פ פ ט | 5

SEARCH AND CIRCLE

Read aloud the sound each letter makes.

One letter on each line makes a different sound. Circle it.

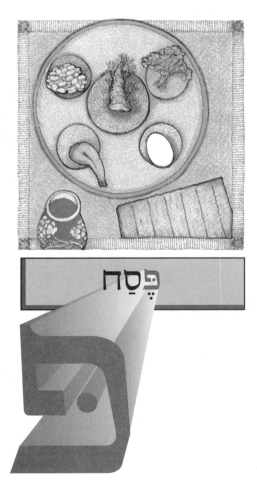

פֶּסַח

70

SOUND MATCH

Read aloud the Hebrew sounds on each line.

Circle the Hebrew that sounds the same as the English in the box.

נְ	נֵ	(נֵ)	נֵ	**NEE**	1
חַ	חִ	חוֹ	חֶ	**ḤAH**	2
פָּ	פֵּ	פַּ	פֹּ	**PEH**	3
טוֹ	טֶ	טַ	טִ	**TOH**	4
עֲ	עִ	עֹ	עָ	**EE**	5
לָ	לַ	לֶ	יוֹ	**YEH**	6

TIC-TAC-TOE

Play tic-tac-toe with a friend. Read the sounds correctly to make an **X** or an **O**.

2

פוֹ	פַּ	פֶּ
פִּ	פֹּ	פָּ
פֶּ	פֹּ	פוֹ

1

טֶ	ט	טָ
טִ	טֹ	טִ
טֹ	טָ	טָ

71

TRACE THE LETTER

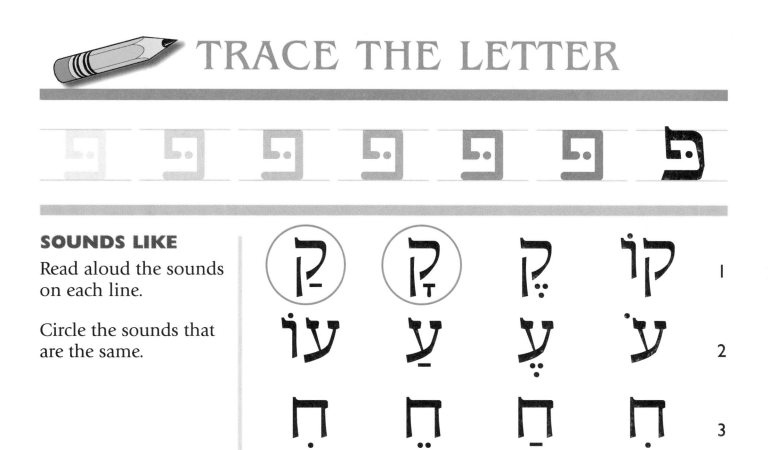

SOUNDS LIKE

Read aloud the sounds on each line.

Circle the sounds that are the same.

קֻו	קֶ	(קָ)	(קַ)	1
עֹו	עֲ	עָ	עֹ	2
חַ	חֶ	חֲ	חִ	3
פֻ	פָ	פֶ	פֵ	4
טֻ	טָ	טַ	טִ	5

DISCOVER THE LETTERS

Color each space that has a dot to see the hidden letter. Say the name and sound of the letters.

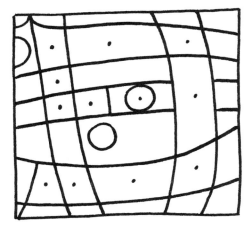

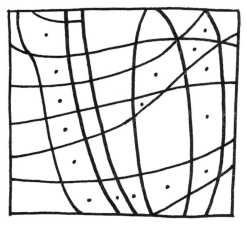

72

SAMECH

Color the Samech

SEARCH AND CIRCLE

Read aloud the sound each letter makes.

One letter on each line makes a different sound. Circle it.

סדור

1   ס   ⊙ח   ס   ס   ס

2   ס   ס   ס   ט   ס

3   ס   ס   ה   ס   ס

4   ס   ת   ס   ס   ס

5   ס   ס   ס   ס   ע

TWINS

Two sounds on each line are the same. Put a box around each of them.

Read aloud the sound.

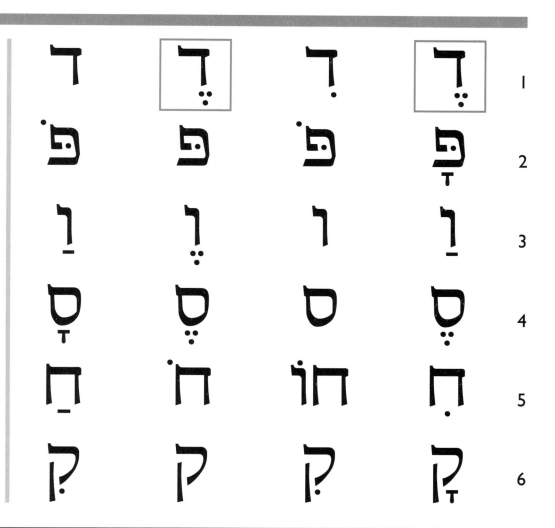

CONNECTIONS

Connect the Hebrew letter to its name. What sound does the letter make?

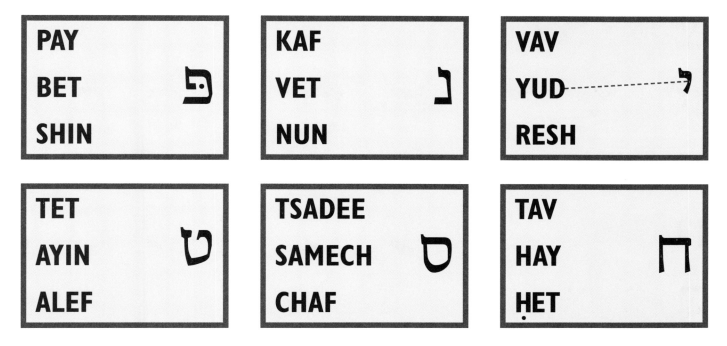

SOUND OFF

Circle the sound each Hebrew letter makes.

Say the sound and the name of the Hebrew letter.

T	V	(M)	L	מ	1
S	N	R	T	ס	2
M	CH	V	P	פ	3
N	M	T	SH	ט	4
H	Y	K	D	י	5

WHAT'S MISSING?

Circle the letter to complete the pattern in each row. Read aloud each line.

(צ)	כ	ק		ק	ר	צ	ק	ר	1
א	פ	ס		ע	ס	פ	ע	ס	2
מ	ח	נ		מ	ל	נ	מ	ל	3
ט	ת	ט		ט	י	ח	ט	י	4
ב	ב	א		ב	ד	א	ב	ד	5

75

Color the Fay

Read aloud the sound each letter makes.

One letter on each line makes a different sound. Circle it.

פ פ (ב) פ פ   1

מ פ פ פ פ   2

פ פ פ ס פ   3

פ פ פ ט פ   4

פ כ פ פ פ   5

SOUND MATCH

Read aloud the Hebrew sounds on each line.

Circle the Hebrew that sounds the same as the English in the box.

חֶ	חֹ	חִ	(חָ)	**HAH**	1
טוֹ	טֶ	טִ	טַ	**TEH**	2
פֶ	פוֹ	פָ	פֵ	**POH**	3
סָ	סֵ	סִ	סֹ	**SEE**	4
קָ	קִ	קֹ	קַ	**KOH**	5
פִ	פֶ	פִ	פָ	**FEE**	6

NAME THE LETTER

Circle the Hebrew letter named in the box.

ר	(ו)	כ	נ	**VAV**	1
כ	ב	ת	פ	**PAY**	2
ס	שׁ	נ	מ	**SAMECH**	3
מ	ע	ק	ח	**KOOF**	4
כ	פ	ב	ל	**FAY**	5
צ	ס	א	ט	**TSADEE**	6

77

ף פ פ פ פ פ פ

COLOR THE SOUNDS

Read aloud the two Hebrew sounds in each balloon. Color the balloon if the two sounds are the same.

How many balloons did you color? _____

רֵ	רֵ	רֵ	רֵ	רֵ	1
פִ	פִ	פִ	פֵ	פֵ	2
נֵ	נֵ	נֵ	נֵ	נֵ	3
סֵ	סֵ	סֵ	סֵ	סֵ	4
פֵ	פֵ	פֵ	פֵ	פֵ	5
תֵ	תֵ	תֵ	תֵ	תֵ	6

79

שֶׁ	(שֶׁ)	שֵׁ	שֵׁ	שֵׁ	1
לִ	לֵ	לֵ	לֵ	לֵ	2
פֵּ	פֵּ	פֵּ	פֵּ	פֵ	3
טֵ	טֵ	טֵ	טָ	טֵ	4
חֵ	חֵ	חֹו	חֵ	חֵ	5
פֵ	פֵ	פֵ	פֵ	פֵ	6
סָ	סֵ	סֵ	סֵ	סֵ	7
אֵ	אֵ	אֵ	אַ	אֵ	8

SEARCH AND CIRCLE

Read aloud the sounds on each line.

One sound on each line is different.

Circle it.

80

Color the Sin

SEARCH AND CIRCLE

Read aloud the sound each letter makes.

One letter on each line makes a different sound. Circle it.

שִׂמְחַת תּוֹרָה

1 שׂ שׂ שׂ שׂ (תְּ)

2 שׂ שׂ שׂ פֻ שׂ

3 שׂ שׂ שׂ כּ שׂ

4 שׂ שׂ שׂ בּ שׂ

5 שׂ שׂ ט שׂ שׂ

81

SOUNDS LIKE

Read aloud the sounds on each line.

Circle the sounds that are the same.

פֻּו	פָ	פֶ	פִּ	1
סֶ	סֶ	סֶ	סִ	2
וְ	וָ	וֹ	וַ	3
פִּ	פֶ	פֶ	פָ	4
שְ	שֻ	שֶ	שַ	5

CONNECTIONS

Connect the Hebrew letter to its name. What sound does the letter make?

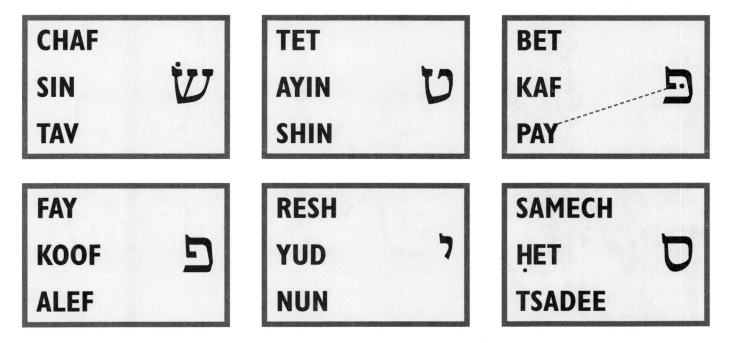

CHAF
SIN   שׁ
TAV

TET
AYIN   ט
SHIN

BET
KAF   פ
PAY

FAY
KOOF   ף
ALEF

RESH
YUD   ל
NUN

SAMECH
ḤET   ס
TSADEE

TRACE THE LETTER

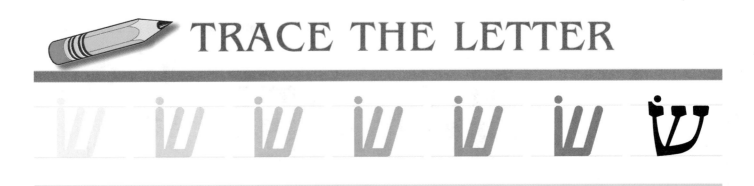

PICTURE MATCH

With what Hebrew sound does the picture begin? Circle the letter.

Color the Gimmel

SEARCH AND CIRCLE

Read aloud the sound each letter makes.

One letter on each line makes a different sound. Circle it.

ג ג ⟨ו⟩ ג ג 1

ג ד ג ג ג 2

ע ג ג ג ג 3

ג ג ג ר ג 4

ג ג ג כ ג 5

TWINS

Read aloud the sounds on each line.

Two sounds on each line are the same. Put a box around each of them.

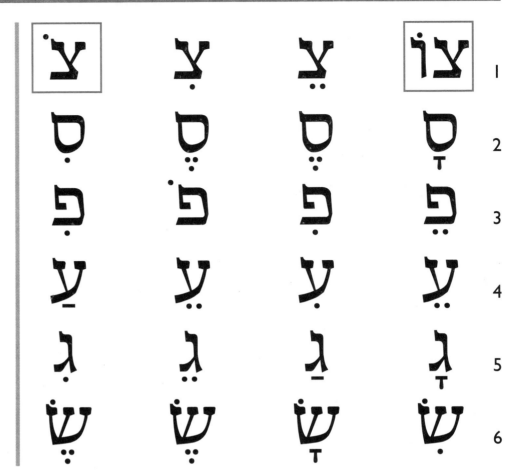

DO THE MATH!

Each letter stands for a number.

5 = הּ	4 = דּ	3 = גּ	2 = בּ	1 = אָ

What are the answers to these problems?

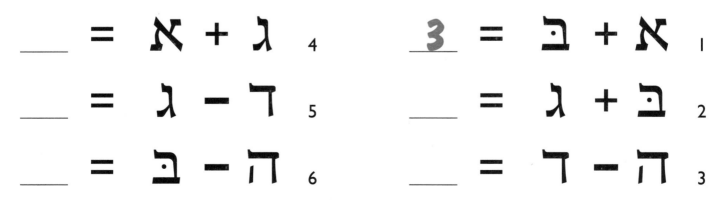

Now make up your own Hebrew math problem.

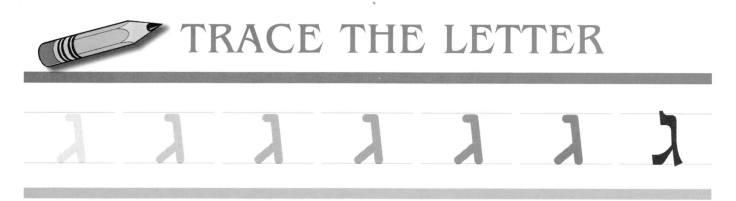

DISCOVER THE LETTERS

Color each space that has a dot to see the hidden letters. Say the name and the sound of the letters.

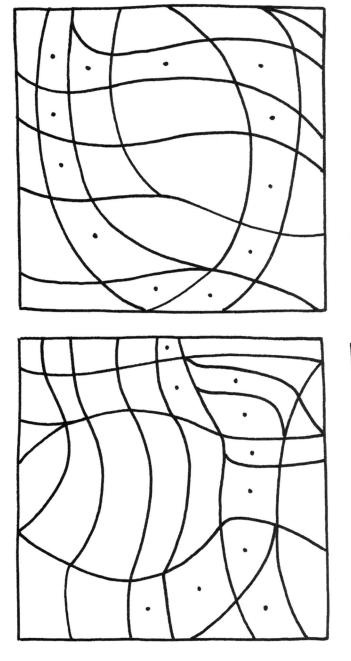

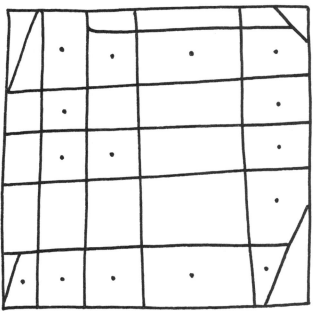

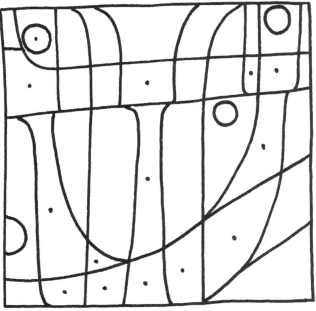

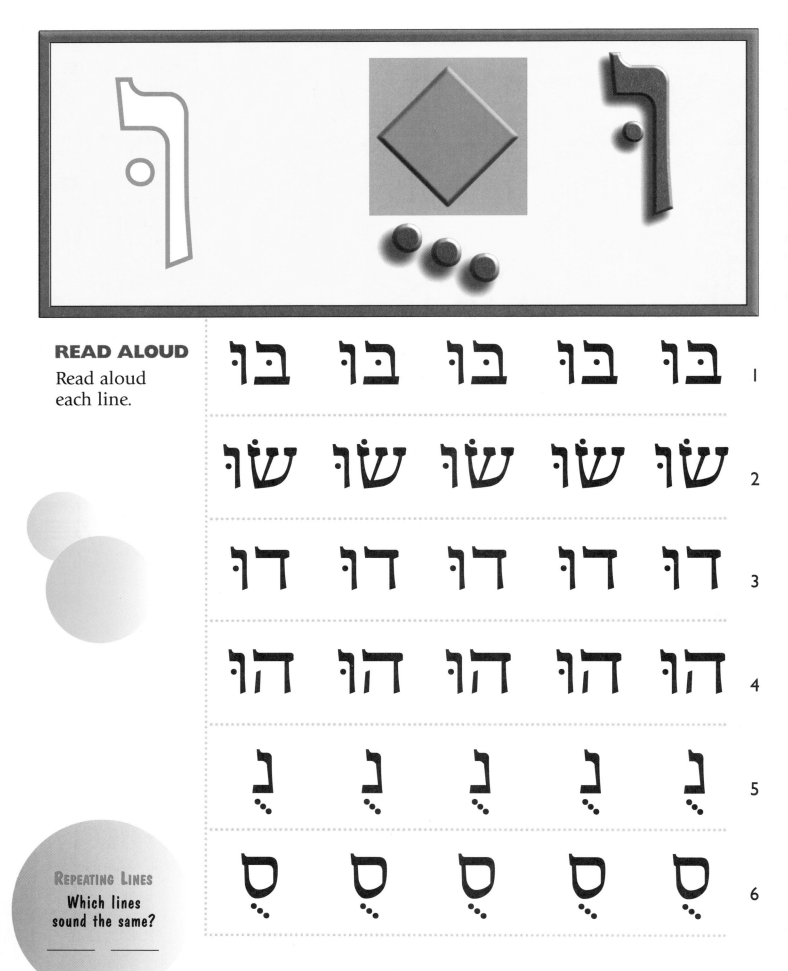

READ ALOUD

Read aloud
each line.

בּוּ	בּוּ	בּוּ	בּוּ	בּוּ	1
שׁוּ	שׁוּ	שׁוּ	שׁוּ	שׁוּ	2
דוּ	דוּ	דוּ	דוּ	דוּ	3
הוּ	הוּ	הוּ	הוּ	הוּ	4
נְ	נְ	נְ	נְ	נְ	5
סְ	סְ	סְ	סְ	סְ	6

REPEATING LINES
Which lines
sound the same?

_____   _____

Read aloud the sounds on each line.

One sound on each line is different. Circle it.

מְ	מְ	מְ	(מֶ)	מֶ	1
רְ	רֶ	רֶ	רֶ	רֶ	2
קוֹ	קֹ	קוֹ	קוֹ	קוֹ	3
פוֹ	פוֹ	פֶ	פוֹ	פוֹ	4
לְ	לְ	לוֹ	לְ	לוֹ	5
גְ	גוֹ	גְ	גוֹ	גְ	6
עְ	עֶ	עַ	עוֹ	עוֹ	7
תְ	תְ	תְ	תְ	תוֹ	8
ווֹ	ווֹ	וְ	וְ	וֹ	9
שׁוֹ	שׁוֹ	שְׁ	שֶׁ	שְׁ	10

ZAYIN

Color the Zayin

SEARCH AND CIRCLE

Read aloud the sound each letter makes.

One letter on each line makes a different sound. Circle it.

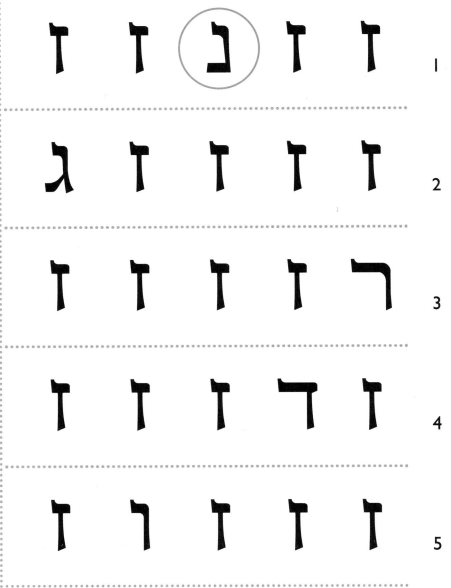

ז ז ב ז ז   1

ג ז ז ז ז   2

ז ז ז ז ר   3

ז ז ז ד ז   4

ז ו ז ז ז   5

SOUND MATCH

Read aloud the Hebrew sounds on each line.

Circle the Hebrew that sounds the same as the English in the box.

POO	1
NEH	2
ZOO	3
FEE	4
SEH	5
GOH	6

WHAT'S MISSING?

Circle the letter to complete the pattern in each row. Read aloud the sounds in each row.

מ ת ס   ___ נ מ ס נ מ   1
ש א ד   ___ ר ק ש ר ק   2
ג ב י   ___ ב א ג ב א   3
ז ל ח   ___ ו ה ז ו ה   4
ט פ צ   ___ ע ט פ ע ט   5

TRACE THE LETTER

ז ז ז ז ז ז ז

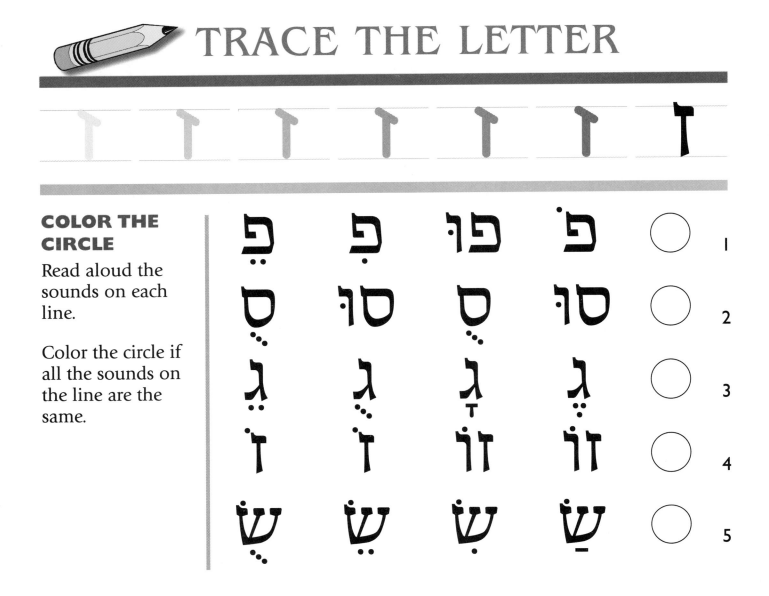

COLOR THE CIRCLE

Read aloud the sounds on each line.

Color the circle if all the sounds on the line are the same.

פֶּ	פֻּ	פוּ	פֹּ	◯ 1
סֻּ	סוּ	סֻ	סוּ	◯ 2
גֶּ	גֶּ	גָ	גֶּ	◯ 3
ז	ז	זוּ	זוּ	◯ 4
שֶׁ	שֶׁ	שׁ	שַׁ	◯ 5

TIC-TAC-TOE

Play tic-tac-toe with a friend. Read the sounds correctly to make an **X** or an **O**.

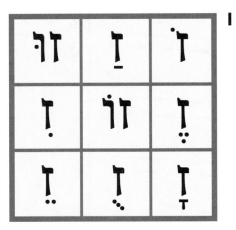

		2
גֶּ	גוּ	גַ
גֹ	גֻ	גוּ
גָ	גֻ	גֶּ

		1
זוּ	ז	ז
ז	זוּ	זֶ
ז	ז	ז

LADDERS

1. Read down one ladder and up the other.
2. Play Ladders with a friend. Taking turns, one player calls out the number of a "rung" and the other player reads the Hebrew sound on that rung. The player scores a point by reading the sound correctly. Write your score here. ______

1 בּוֹ
2 לֶ
3 יַ
4 שֵׁ
5 דִ
6 מֶ
7 סֵ
8 צַ
9 כֶ
10 טִ
11 פֶּ
12 קֵ
13 פוֹ
14 רֶ
15 זוּ
16 אַ
17 חֶ
18 בִ
19 תֹ
20 נָ
21 כֵּ
22 הִ

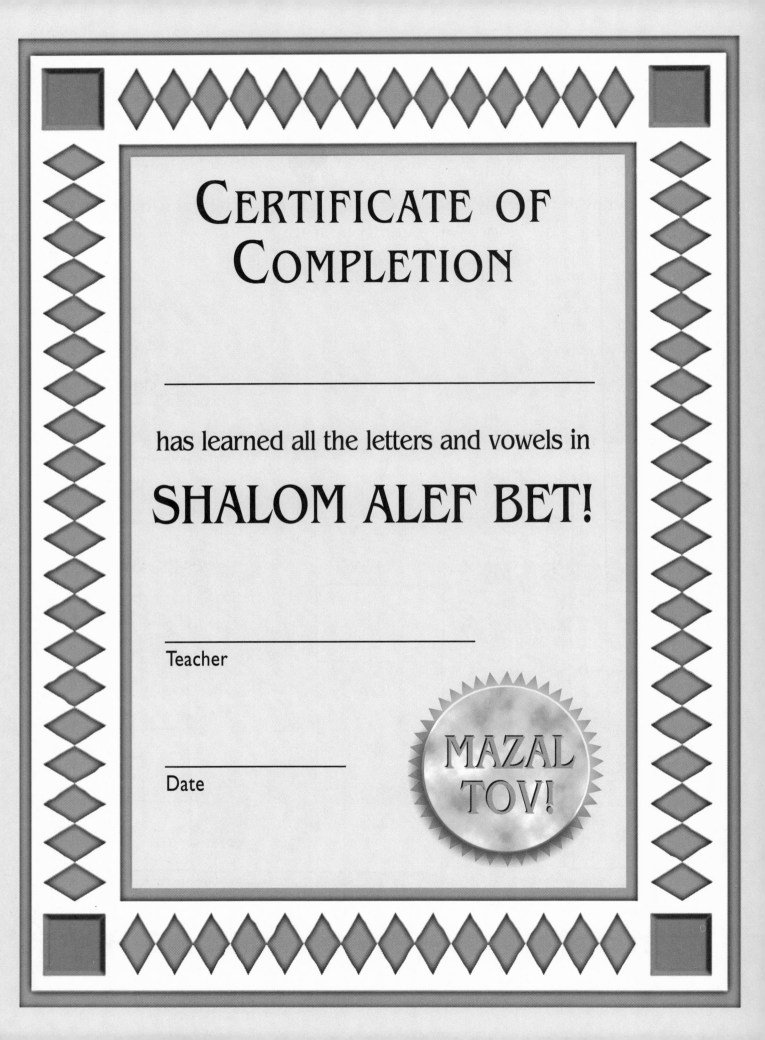

CERTIFICATE OF COMPLETION

_____

has learned all the letters and vowels in

SHALOM ALEF BET!

_____

Teacher

_____

Date

MAZAL TOV!

ALEF BET BOARD GAME

Play the game with a friend.

1. Each person places a button on "Start."

2. Flip a penny. If the penny lands on "heads," move your button two spaces. If it lands on "tails," move your button one space.

3. If you land on a LETTER, say the name and sound of the letter. If you land on a VOWEL, say the sound of the vowel. If you land on a PICTURE, say the Hebrew word for the picture. (If you get stuck, have your friend help you.)

4. If you land on a space with a STAR, give your answer, then take another turn!

5. The first player to reach the ALEF BET HOUSE wins!

ALEF BET CHART

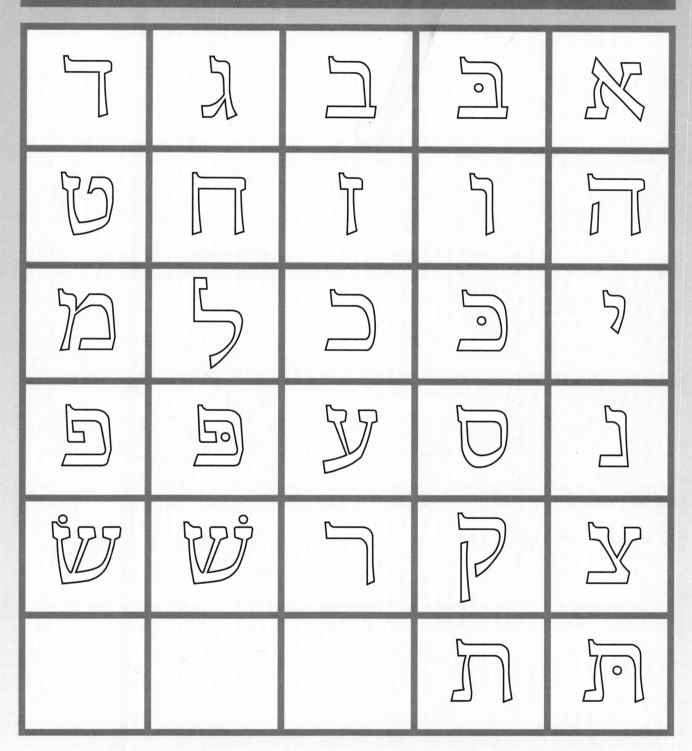

SEARCH AND CIRCLE

Read aloud the sound each letter makes.

One letter on each line makes a different sound. Circle it.

יִשְׂרָאֵל

ן	י	י	י	י	1
ל	ל	י	ר	י	2
ל	כ	י	י	ל	3
ל	ל	י	י	ה	4
ל	י	ד	י	ל	5

59

Shalom Alef Bet!

A Pre-Primer for Shalom Uvrachah

Pearl Tarnor

BEHRMAN HOUSE, INC.

Book and Cover Design: Irving S. Berman

Electronic Composition and Page Production:
21st Century Publishing and Communications, Inc.

Illustrations: Bonnie Gordon-Lucas

Activity Art: Deborah Zemke

Project Manager: Terry S. Kaye

Copyright © 2000 Behrman House, Inc.
Springfield, New Jersey
www.behrmanhouse.com
ISBN 0-87441-693-0
Manufactured in the United States of America

Dear Hebrew student,

Welcome to the Alef Bet!

In this book you will make friends with the Hebrew letters. You will learn their names and the sounds they make, and you will practice writing them. You will also learn important Hebrew words to use in school or at home. By the end of the year, you'll be able to say "Israel," "tree," and "Jewish star" in Hebrew! You'll know the names of Jewish holidays, and the objects in your synagogue, such as the Holy Ark.

While you are learning, you can have fun finding twin letters, completing patterns, coloring to find a hidden letter, and playing board games. You'll even do math using Hebrew letters!

You are on your way to becoming a Hebrew reader. Good luck and have fun as you go!

BET

Color the Bet

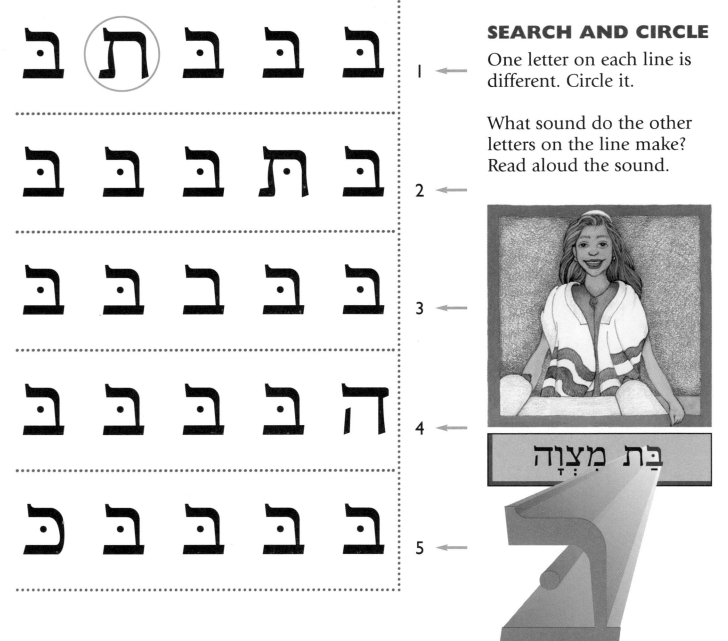

SEARCH AND CIRCLE

One letter on each line is different. Circle it.

What sound do the other letters on the line make? Read aloud the sound.

1 ←

2 ←

3 ←

4 ←

5 ←

בַּת מִצְוָה

4

SOUNDS LIKE

Circle the Hebrew letters that are the same on each line. Read aloud the sound.

בַּר מִצְוָה

ת	(בּ)	(בּ)	1 ←
בּ	כ	בּ	2 ←
בּ	בּ	ה	3 ←
ת	בּ	בּ	4 ←

PUT A CHECK

Put a ✓ on the line if all the letters are the same.

Put an ✗ if they are different.

בּ	בּ	בּ	בּ	✓ 1 ←
בּ	בּ	בּ	כ	___ 2 ←
בּ	בּ	בּ	ת	___ 3 ←
ת	בּ	ת	ת	___ 4 ←

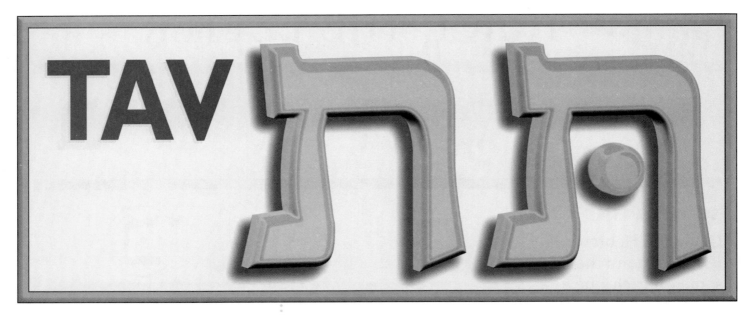

TAV

SEARCH AND CIRCLE

Read aloud the sound each letter makes.

One letter on each line makes a different sound. Circle it.

תּוֹרָה

1 → תּ בּ תּ תּ
2 → תּ ת ת בּ
3 → בּ בּ ת בּ
4 → בּ תּ בּ בּ
5 → בּ ת תּ ת

TRACE THE LETTER

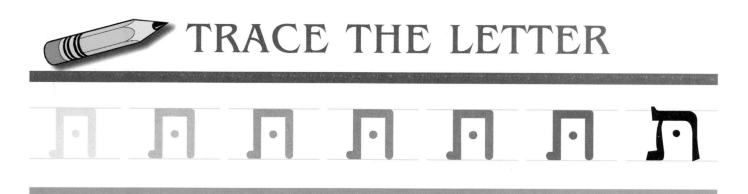

CONNECTIONS

Connect the Hebrew letter to its name. What sound does the letter make?

PUT A CHECK

Put a ✓ on the line if all the letters are the same. Put an ✗ if they are different. Read aloud the sounds on each line.

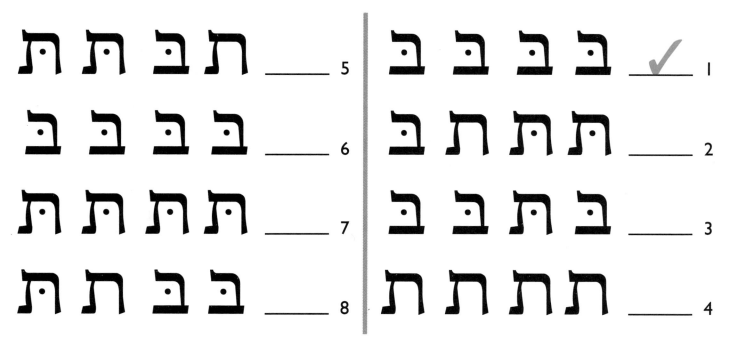

Color the Shin

שׁ שׁ שׁ שׁ (בּ) שׁ   1

שׂ שׂ תּ שׂ שׂ שׂ   2

שׁ שׁ שׁ שׁ תּ   3

שׂ שׂ שׂ בּ שׁ שׁ   4

בּ שׁ בּ בּ שׁ בּ   5

SEARCH AND CIRCLE

Read aloud the sound each letter makes.

One letter on each line makes a different sound. Circle it.

שַׁבָּת

8

TRACE THE LETTER

שׁ שׁ שׁ שׁ שׁ שׁ שׁ שׁ

TWINS

Read aloud the sounds on each line.

Two letters on each line are the same. Put a box around each of them.

שׁוֹפָר

בּ	שׁ	בּ	תּ	1
תּ	בּ	שׁ	תּ	2
תּ	שׁ	בּ	שׁ	3
שׁ	בּ	תּ	תּ	4

NAME THE LETTER

Circle the Hebrew letter named in the box.

שָׁלוֹם

TAV	בּ	שׁ	תּ	1
SHIN	שׁ	תּ	בּ	2
BET	תּ	בּ	שׁ	3
TAV	בּ	תּ	שׁ	4

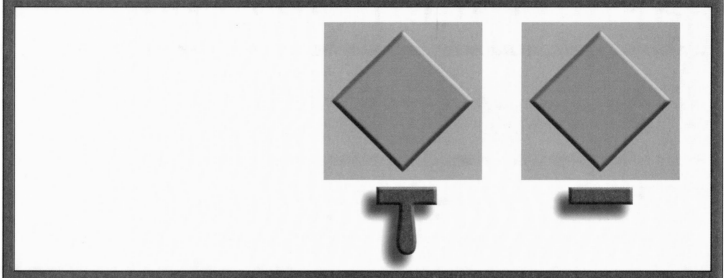

READ ALOUD
Read aloud each line.

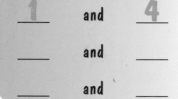
שֶׁמֶשׁ

REPEATING LINES
Which lines sound the same?

___1___ and ___4___

_____ and _____

_____ and _____

בְּ בְ בְּ בֶ בַּ 1

תַ תָ תַ תָ תָ 2

שַׁ שָׁ שַׁ שָׁ שָׁ 3

בָּ בַ בָּ בְ בַּ 4

שָׁ שָׁ שָׁ שָׁ שָׁ 5

תָ תָ תָ תָ תָ 6

SOUND MATCH

Read aloud the Hebrew sounds on each line.

Circle the Hebrew that sounds the same as the English in the box.

תָּ	שׁ	(תָּ)	בָּ	תַּ	T	1
שׁ	(שָׁ)	בַּ	תָּ	תָּ	SHAH	2
תַּ	בָּ	שׁ	(בַּ)	שׁ	BAH	3
שׁ	(שׁ)	תָּ	שָׁ	בָּ	SH	4
בּ	בַּ	(תָּ)	שָׁ	תָּ	TAH	5

PICTURE MATCH

Connect the letter to its matching picture.

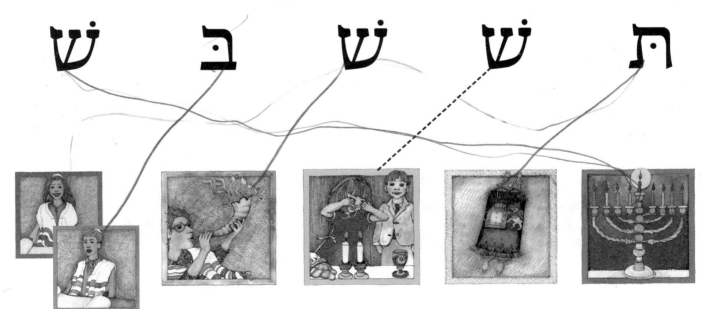

11

Color the Mem

SEARCH AND CIRCLE

Read aloud the sound each letter makes.

One letter on each line makes a different sound. Circle it.

מְזוּזָה

1   מ מ מ (בּ) מ

2   מ מ מ שׂ מ

3   מ מ ת מ מ

4   ת ת ת מ ת

5   ב מ מ מ מ

12

DISCOVER THE LETTER

Color each space that has a dot to see the hidden letter.

Say the name and sound of the letter.

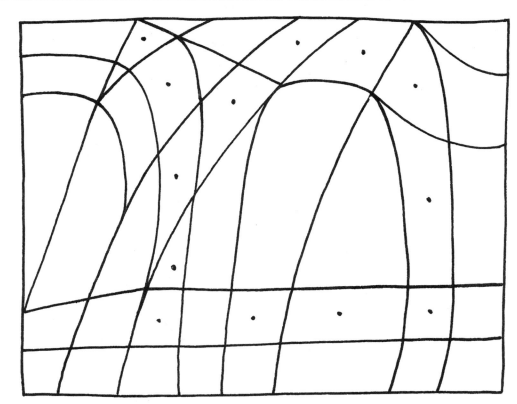

SOUNDS LIKE

Read aloud the sound each letter makes.

Circle the letters that are the same on each line.

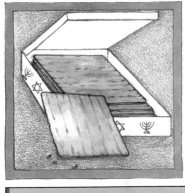

מַצָּה

How many times did you circle מ? _____

שׁ	תּ	מ	שׂ		1
ב	מ	בּ	תּ		2
מ	שׁ	תּ	מ		3
תּ	תּ	בּ	שׁ		4
מ	שׁ	מ	ב		5

13

מ מ מ מ מ מ מ **מ**

מַ	מַ	מַ	מַ	✔ 1
תָ	תָ	תָ	תָ	___ 2
בַ	בֵ	בַ	בַ	___ 3
שָׁ	שָׁ	שָׁ	שָׁ	___ 4
תָ	תָ	תָ	תָ	___ 5
מַ	מָ	מָ	מַ	___ 6

PUT A CHECK

Read aloud the sounds on each line.

Put a ✔ on the line if all the sounds are the same.

Put an ✗ if they are different.

מָגֵן דָּוִד

REPEATING LINES

Which lines sound the same?

__1__ and __6__

___ and ___

Color the Lamed

SEARCH AND CIRCLE

Read aloud the sound each letter makes.

One letter on each line makes a different sound. Circle it.

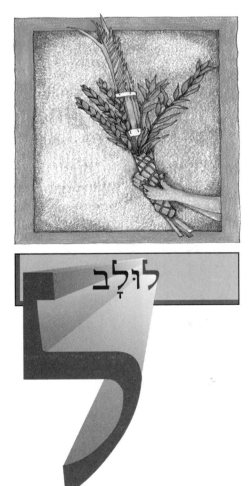

לוּלָב

ל ל ל ל מ 1

ל ל ל שׁ ל 2

ל ל ל ת 3

ל ל ל ב ל 4

ל ל ל מ ל 5

15

NAME THE LETTER

Circle the Hebrew letter named in the box.

מ	ⓑ	שׁ	**BET**	1
ת	ל	ⓜ	**MEM**	2
ⓈΨ	ת	בּ	**SHIN**	3
שׁ	מ	ⓛ	**LAMED**	4
ⓉΤ	ל	מ	**TAV**	5

SOUNDS LIKE

Read aloud the sounds on each line.

Circle the sounds that are the same.

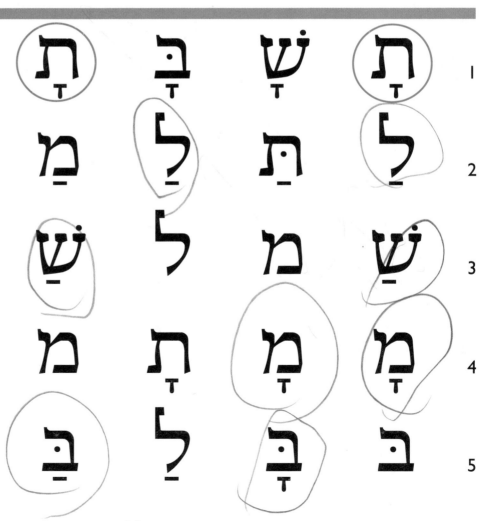

Ⓣתָ	בְּ	שָׁ	Ⓣתָ	1
מַ	Ⓛלְ	תַ	Ⓛל	2
Ⓢשֶׁ	ל	מ	שֶׁ	3
מ	תָ	ⓜמָ	ⓜמָ	4
ⓑבְ	ל	ⓑבָּ	בּ	5

16

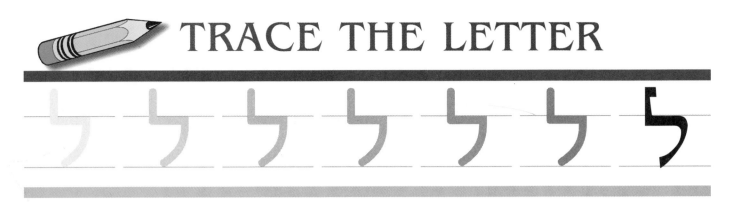

TRACE THE LETTER

WHAT'S MISSING?

Circle the letter to complete the pattern in each row.

Read aloud the sounds in each row.

Color the Kaf

כ כ (ת) כ כ   1

ב כ כ כ כ   2

כ כ מ כ כ   3

כ כ ל כ כ   4

כ כ כ שׁ כ   5

SEARCH AND CIRCLE

Read aloud the sound each letter makes.

One letter on each line makes a different sound. Circle it.

כִּפָּה

SOUND OFF

Circle the sound each Hebrew letter makes.

Say the sound and the name of the Hebrew letter.

(SH)	L	T	M	שׁ	1
B	M	K	T	כ	2
K	T	B	SH	ת	3
B	L	SH	M	מ	4
L	K	M	T	ל	5

TWINS

Read aloud the sounds on each line.

Two sounds on each line are the same. Put a box around each of them.

19

TRACE THE LETTER

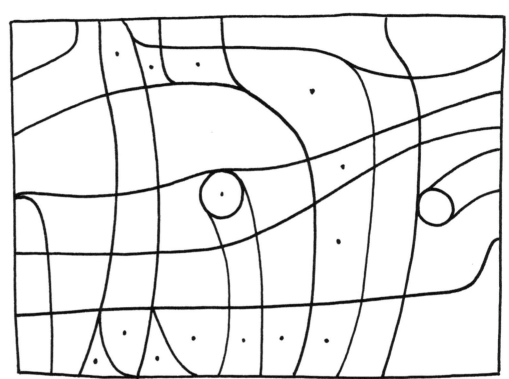

DISCOVER THE LETTER

Color each space that has a dot to see the hidden letter.

Say the name and sound of the letter.

CONNECTIONS

Connect each Hebrew letter to its name. What sound does each letter make?

| LAMED | מ | | KAF | כ | | SHIN | ת |
| MEM | ל | | BET | ב | | TAV | שׁ |

HAY

Color the Hay

SEARCH AND CIRCLE

Read aloud the sound each letter makes.

One letter on each line makes a different sound. Circle it.

הַגָּדָה

1   ה   (ת)   ה   ה   ה

2   מ   ה   ה   ה   ה

3   ה   ה   ה   ה   ת

4   ה   ה   ה   ל   ה

5   ה   ה   ה   ה   שׁ

NAME THE LETTER

Circle the Hebrew letter named in the box.

מ	ה	ת	TAV	1
ל	שׁ	מ	LAMED	2
ת	ה	שׁ	HAY	3
ב	כ	תּ	KAF	4
מ	ל	ת	MEM	5

COLOR THE CIRCLE

Read aloud the sounds on each line.

Color the circle if all the sounds on the line are the same.

כָּ	כָּ	כָּ	כָּ	⬤	1
לְ	לְ	לְ	לְ	◯	2
שֶׁ	שָׁ	שֶׁ	שֶׁ	◯	3
הָ	הַ	הָ	הַ	◯	4
בָ	בַ	בַ	בָ	◯	5

22

TRACE THE LETTER

ה ה ה ה ה ה

SOUND MATCH

Read aloud the Hebrew sounds on each line.

Circle the Hebrew that sounds the same as the English in the box.

בְּ בְ	שׁ שׂ	⊙ בְּ	כ	**B** 1
מְ מָ	מ	לְ	תָ	**MAH** 2
כְ כ	כְ	בְ בָ	בְ	**KAH** 3
שׁ	לְ	תָ	ל	**L** 4
ה ה	תָ	ה	תַ	**HAH** 5

THREE IN A ROW

Draw a line to connect the three KAH sounds.

Draw a line to connect the three HAH sounds.

Draw a line to connect the three LAH sounds.

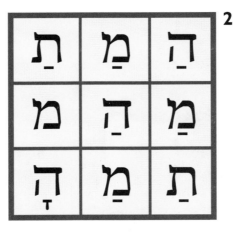

3

בְּ	הַ	תָ
בְּ	הַ	תָ
כְ	כ	כְ

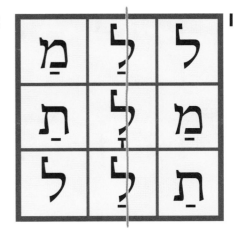

2

הַ	מַ	תָ
מ	הַ	מ
תָ	מ	תַ

1

ל	לְ	מַ
מ	לְ	תָ
תָ	לְ	ל

23

Color the Resh

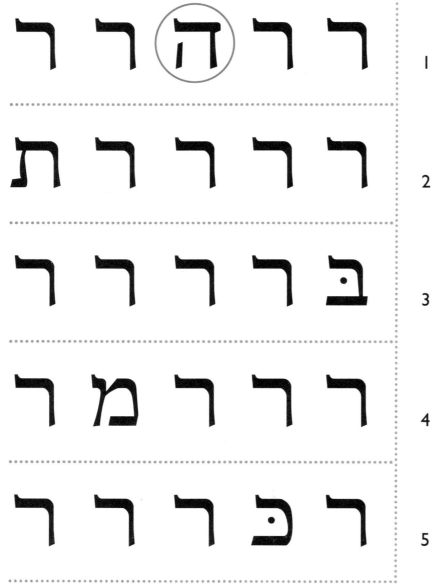

ר	ר	(ה)	ר	ר	1
ר	ר	ר	ר	ת	2
ר	ר	ר	ר	בּ	3
ר	ר	ר	מ	ר	4
ר	ר	ר	כּ	ר	5

SEARCH AND CIRCLE

Read aloud the sound each letter makes.

One letter on each line makes a different sound. Circle it.

רֹאשׁ הַשָּׁנָה

24

CONNECTIONS

Connect each Hebrew letter to its name. What sound does each letter make?

KAF	ל
TAV	כַ
LAMED	תָ

MEM	ר
HAY	מַ
RESH	הַ

SHIN	בּ
BET	תָ
TAV	שַׁ

SOUNDS LIKE

Read aloud the sounds on each line.

Circle the sounds that are the same.

TRACE THE LETTER

ר ר ר ר ר ר ר ר

H	(B)	L	K	ב	1
M	T	SH	R	שׁ	2
K	R	B	L	ל	3
R	H	M	T	ר	4
T	M	L	K	מ	5
L	R	H	SH	ה	6
K	M	L	B	כ	7
SH	T	B	H	ת	8

SOUND OFF

Circle the sound each Hebrew letter makes.

Say the sound and the name of the Hebrew letter.

26

CHAF

Color the Chaf

SEARCH AND CIRCLE

Read aloud the sound each letter makes.

One letter on each line makes a different sound. Circle it.

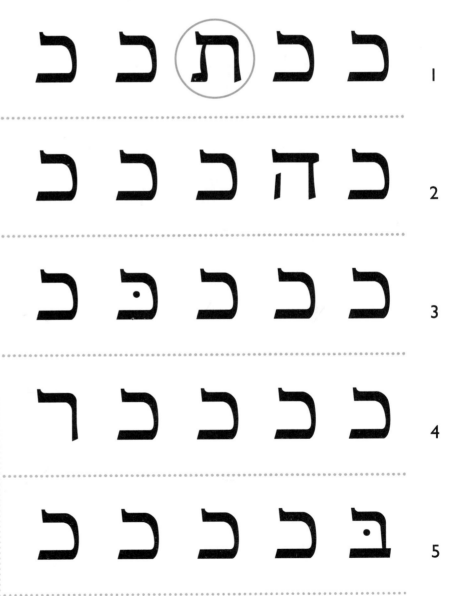

כ כ ת כ כ   1

כ ה כ כ כ   2

כ כ כ כֹ כ   3

כ כ כ כ ר   4

בֹ כ כ כ כ   5

COLOR THE CIRCLE

Read aloud the sounds on each line.

Color the circle if all the sounds on the line are the same.

שָׁ	שָׁ	שָׁ	שָׁ	●	1
כָּ	כָּ	כַּ	כָּ	○	2
הָ	ה	ה	ה	○	3
כָּ	כָּ	כָּ	כָּ	○	4
מָ	מ	מ	מָ	○	5

SOUND MATCH

Read aloud the Hebrew sounds on each line.

Circle the Hebrew that sounds the same as the English in the box.

הַ	תַּ	רַ	תָּ	TAH	1
רָ	כָּ	הַ	ר	RAH	2
כַ	תַ	כַ	רָ	CHAH	3
ה	רַ	תַ	הַ	HAH	4
ל	לָ	שָׁ	מָ	LAH	5
מַ	כַ	מ	תַ	MAH	6

28

TRACE THE LETTER

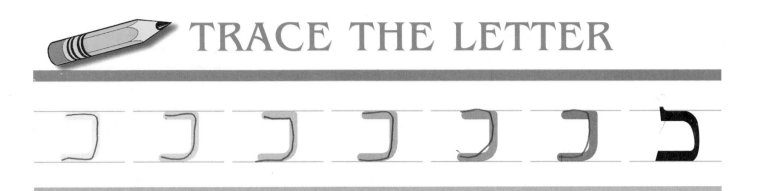

כ כ כ כ כ כ כ כ כ

WHAT'S MISSING?

Circle the letter to complete the pattern in each row.

Read aloud the sounds in each row.

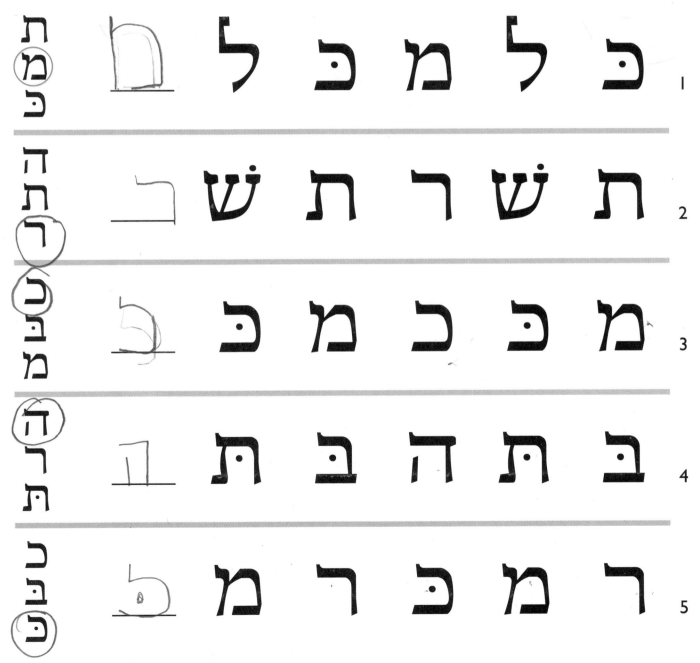

29

Color the Vet

VET

ב ב ב (ת) ב |

ב ב בּ כ ב   2

ב ב ב ב ל   3

ב ר ב ב ב   4

ב בּ ב ב ב   5

SEARCH AND CIRCLE

Read aloud the sound each letter makes.

One letter on each line makes a different sound. Circle it.

On which line did you find בּ? _____

On which line did you find ב? _____

30

NAME THE LETTER

Circle the Hebrew letter named in the box.

ל	מ	ה	ה	**MEM** 1
שׁ	כ	בּ	כ	**SHIN** 2
ה	ת	כ	ת	**CHAF** 3
ה	ר	ת	ת	**RESH** 4
ב	בּ	כ	כ	**VET** 5

TWINS

Read aloud the sounds on each line.

Two sounds on each line are the same. Put a box around each of them.

כֵּ	כֵּ	בֵּ	כָּ	1
הֵ	רָ	הָ	תָּ	2
בֵ	רָ	בָ	רָ	3
רֵ	רָ	תָ	רָ	4
כֵ	בָ	כֵ	כָ	5

31

ב נ ב נ ב נ ב נ ב נ ב

DISCOVER THE LETTER

Color each space that has a dot to see the hidden letter.

Say the name and sound of the letter.

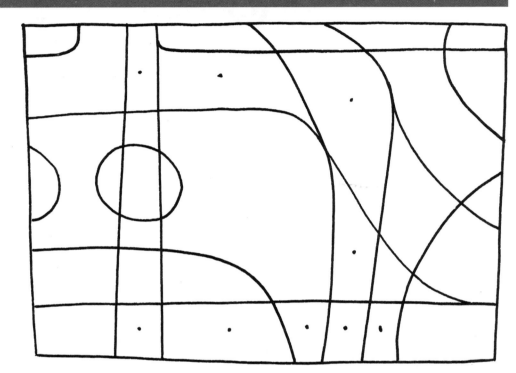

THREE IN A ROW

Draw a line to connect the three VAH sounds.

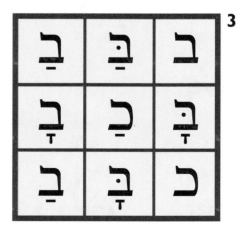

Draw a line to connect the three CHAH sounds.

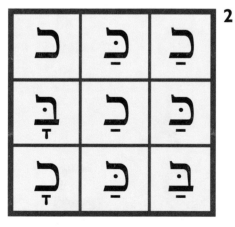

Draw a line to connect the three SHAH sounds.

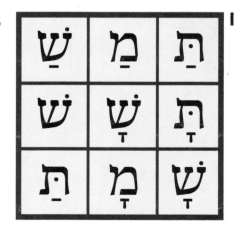

DALET

Color the Dalet

SEARCH AND CIRCLE

Read aloud the sound each letter makes.

One letter on each line makes a different sound. Circle it.

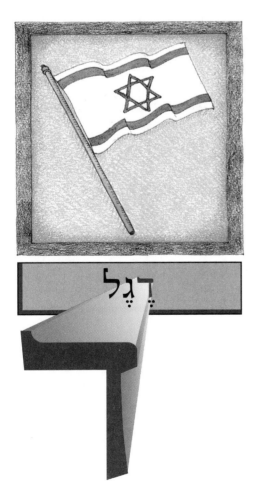

דֶגֶל

ד ד ד (ב) ד ‏1

ת ד ד ד ד ‏2

ד ד ד כ ד ‏3

ד ד ה ד ד ‏4

ד ד ד ד ר ‏5

WHAT'S THAT SOUND?

Circle the English letter that has the sound of the Hebrew letter in the box.

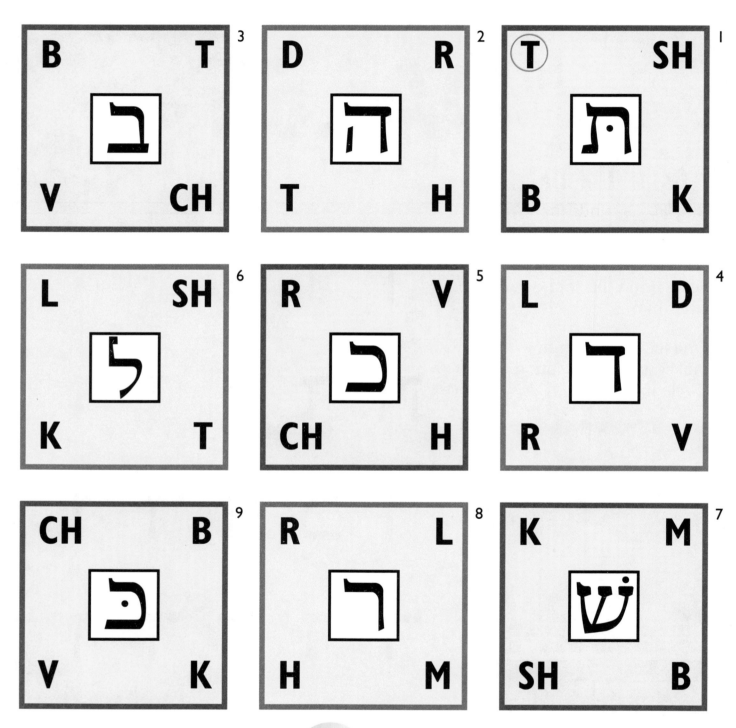

דדדדדדדד

SOUNDS LIKE

Read aloud the sounds on each line.

Circle the sounds that are the same.

תָ	(מָ)	מ	(מַ)	1
בָ	דָ	כָ	בָ	2
ד	כַ	רַ	רַ	3
כַ	בָ	כָ	כֵ	4
הָ	כַ	הַ	תַ	5
הַ	דַ	דָ	רַ	6

35

BINGO FOR ONE

Write the number of the English sound in its matching Hebrew box.
Try to fill the entire board!

1. SH
2. RAH
3. KAH
4. R

5. HAH
6. ~~TAH~~
7. D
8. VAH

9. LAH
10. CHAH
11. MAH
12. DAH

13. BAH
14. T
15. SHAH
16. M

ALEF

Color the Alef

SEARCH AND CIRCLE

One letter on each line is different. Circle it.

Say the sound.

אֲרוֹן הַקֹּדֶשׁ

א א (מ) א א ‎1

ל א א א ‎2

א א א ת א ‎3

א ה א א ‎4

א א א כ ‎5

37

COLOR THE CIRCLE

Read aloud the sounds on each line.

Color the circle if all the sounds on the line are the same.

CONNECTIONS

Connect each Hebrew letter to its name. What sound does the letter make?

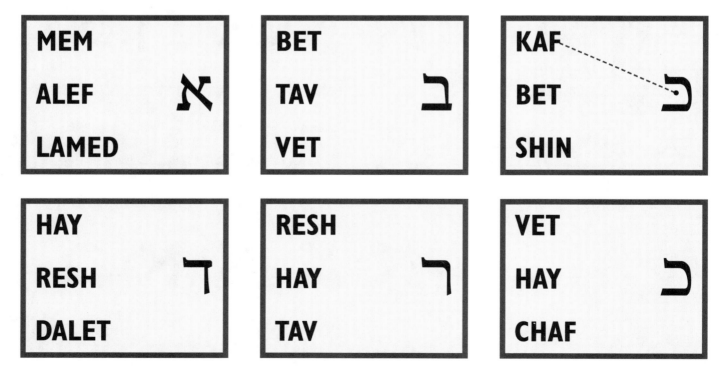

MEM	BET	KAF
ALEF א	TAV ב	BET כ
LAMED	VET	SHIN

HAY	RESH	VET
RESH ד	HAY ר	HAY כ
DALET	TAV	CHAF

38

TRACE THE LETTER

אּ אּ אּ אּ אּ אּ אּ **א**

SOUND MATCH

Read aloud the Hebrew sounds on each line.

Circle the Hebrew letters that sound the same as the English in the box.

BAH	1
DAH	2
VAH	3
CHAH	4
AH	5

THREE IN A ROW

Draw a line to connect the three AH sounds.

Draw a line to connect the three DAH sounds.

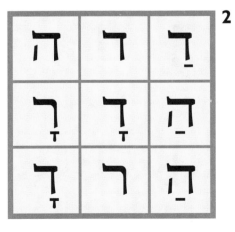

Draw a line to connect the three LAH sounds.

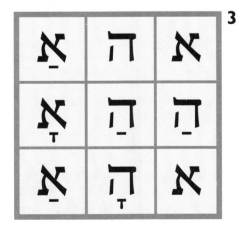

39

VAV

Color the Vav

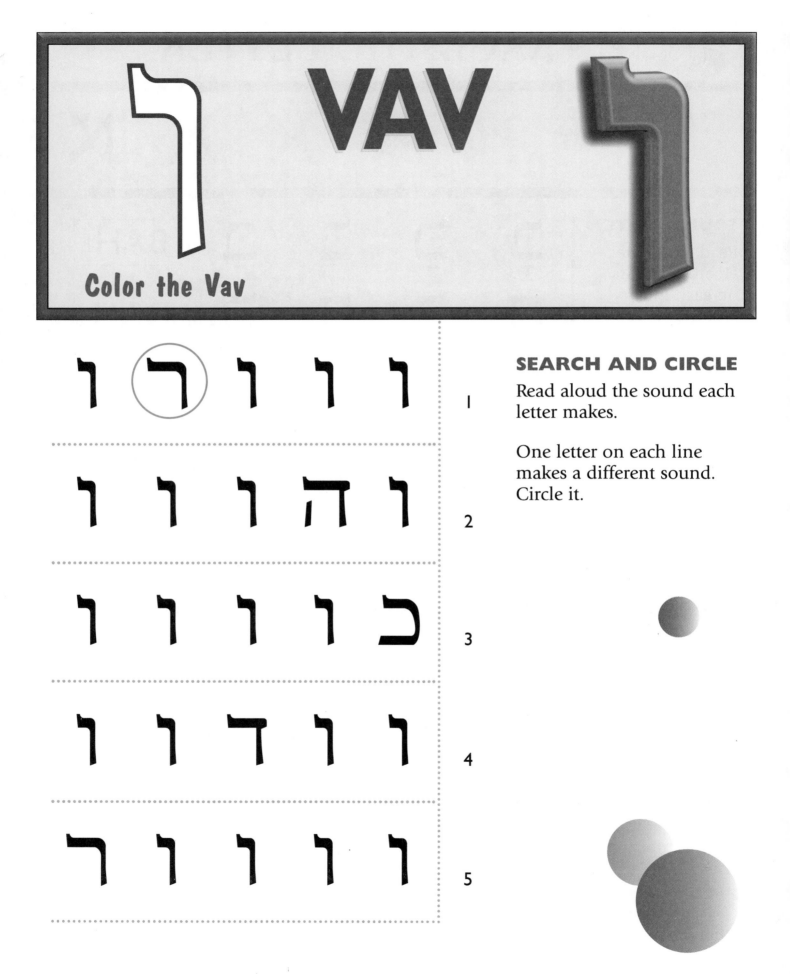

SEARCH AND CIRCLE

Read aloud the sound each letter makes.

One letter on each line makes a different sound. Circle it.

1

2

3

4

5

40

TRACE THE LETTER

TWINS

Read aloud the sounds on each line.

Two sounds on each line are the same. Put a box around each of them.

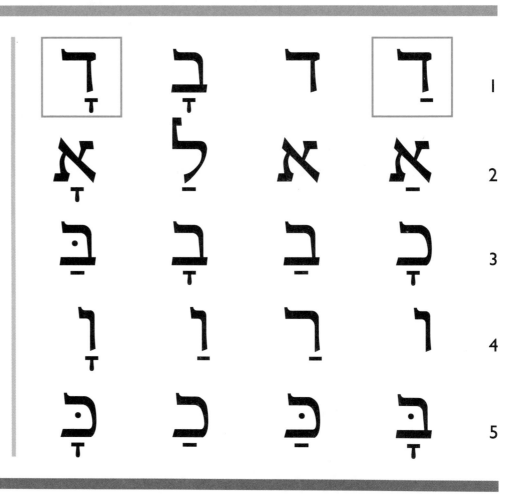

דָ	דָ	בְּ	דָ	1
אָ	אָ	לְ	אָ	2
כָ	בָ	בָ	בְּ	3
בָ	רְ	וְ	וְ	4
בָ	כֶ	כָ	כָ	5

DISCOVER THE LETTER

Connect the dots to see the hidden letters. What is the sound of each letter?

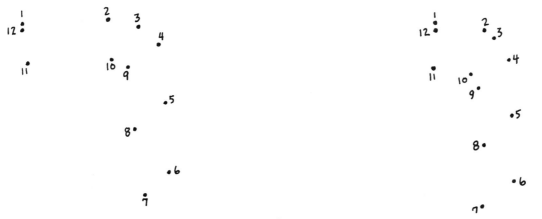

41

Color the Koof

ק	(ל)	ק	ק	ק	**1**
ק	ק	ת	ק	ק	**2**
ק	ק	ק	ק	א	**3**
ק	ק	ק	מ	ק	**4**
כ	ק	ק	ק	ק	**5**

SEARCH AND CIRCLE

Read aloud the sound each letter makes.

One letter on each line makes a different sound. Circle it.

קָדוּשׁ

42

SOUND OFF

Circle the sound each Hebrew letter makes.

Say the sound and the name of the Hebrew letter.

M	(R)	V	T	ר	1
V	H	L	D	ו	2
D	T	K	B	ק	3
R	L	M	D	ד	4
CH	K	H	V	כ	5

SOUNDS LIKE

Read aloud the sounds on each line.

Circle the Hebrew sounds that are the same.

ב	(לָ)	הָ	(לַ)	ל	1
אָ	הַ	א	מָ	אַ	2
ר	וְ	ו	רָ	וְ	3
ד	קָ	ה	ק	קָ	4
בָּ	ב	כָ	כָ	כ	5

43

TRACE THE LETTER

ק ק ק ק ק ק ק

PICTURE MATCH

With what Hebrew sound does the picture begin? Circle the letter.

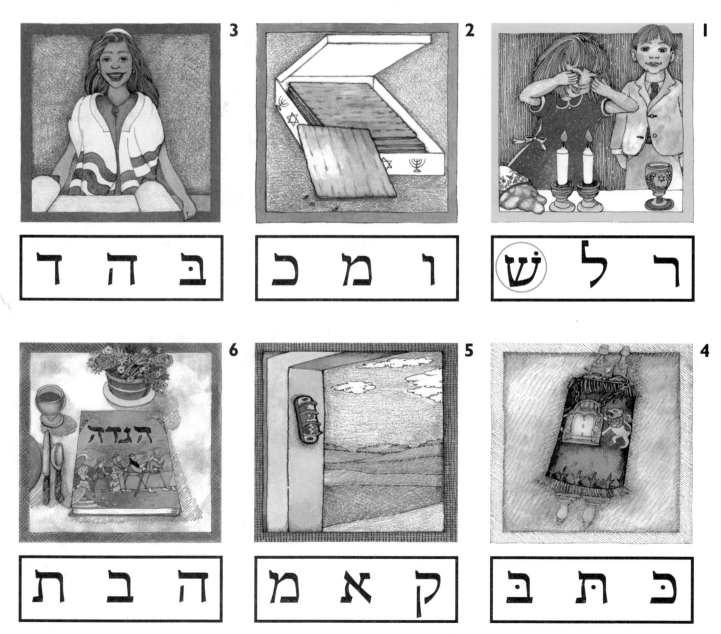

3

ד ה ב

2

ו מ כ

1

ר ל שׁ

6

ת ב ה

5

ק א מ

4

ב ת כ

TSADEE צ

Color the Tsadee

SEARCH AND CIRCLE

Read aloud the sound each letter makes.

One letter on each line makes a different sound. Circle it.

צְדָקָה

1   צ   צ   צ   ⟨ק⟩

2   צ   צ   צ   ל   צ

3   ת   צ   צ   צ

4   צ   צ   מ   צ

5   צ   שׁ   צ   צ

45

COLOR THE CIRCLE

Read aloud the sounds on each line.

Color the circle if all the sounds on the line are the same.

אָ	אַ	אָ	אַ	●	1
ד	ד	ד	ר	○	2
צָ	צַ	צָ	צָ	○	3
וָ	ר	וָ	וָ	○	4
בָ	בָ	בַ	בָ	○	5
קָ	ק	ק	קָ	○	6

WHAT'S MISSING?

Circle the letter to complete the pattern in each row. Read aloud the sounds in each row.

ה (ד) ת		ב ב בּ ד ב בּ	1
כ ב ת		ו כ ה ו ה	2
מ א שׁ		ל כ מ ל כּ	3
ל ר ו		ק צ ר ק צ	4
א צ ת		שׁ א ת שׁ א	5

46

TRACE THE LETTER

PATHWAYS

Find the path that leads each letter to the picture beginning with the same sound as the letter.

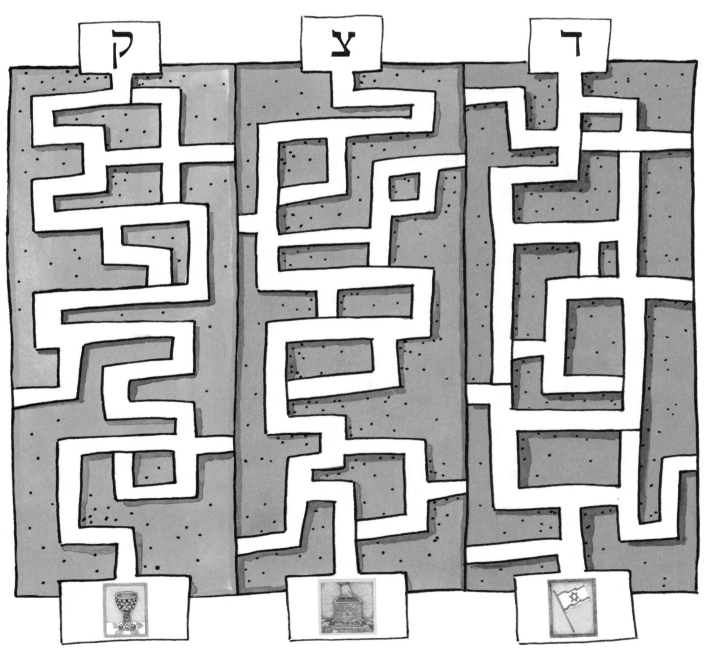

Read aloud each line.

בְּ	בְּ	בְּ	בְּ	בְּ	1
שָׁ	שָׁ	שָׁ	שָׁ	שָׁ	2
תָּ	תָּ	תָּ	תָּ	תָּ	3
מְ	מְ	מְ	מְ	מְ	4
לְ	לְ	לְ	לְ	לְ	5
כְ	כְ	כְ	כְ	כְ	6

SEARCH AND CIRCLE

Read aloud the sounds on each line.

One letter on each line makes a different sound. Circle it.

On which lines did you circle "vah"?

_____ _____

הָ	הָ	הָ	הַ	הָ	1
רְ	רְ	רָ	רְ	רְ	2
כְ	כַ	כְ	כְ	כְ	3
בְ	בְ	בָ	בְ	בְ	4
דְ	דְ	דְ	דְ	דַ	5
אְ	אְ	אָ	אְ	אְ	6
וְ	וָ	וְ	וְ	וְ	7
קְ	קְ	קַ	קְ	קְ	8
צְ	צְ	צְ	צְ	צָ	9

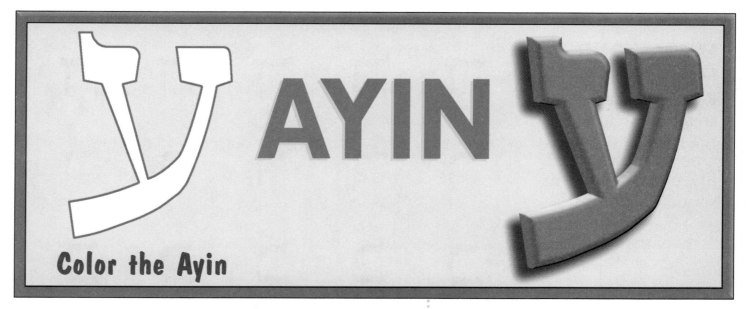

Color the Ayin

ע ע ע ע (ה) ⟵ 1

ע ע ק ע ע ⟵ 2

ע ע ע ד ⟵ 3

ע ע ע צ ע ⟵ 4

ע ע ע א ע ⟵ 5

SEARCH AND CIRCLE

One letter on each line is different. Circle it.

Say the name of the letter.

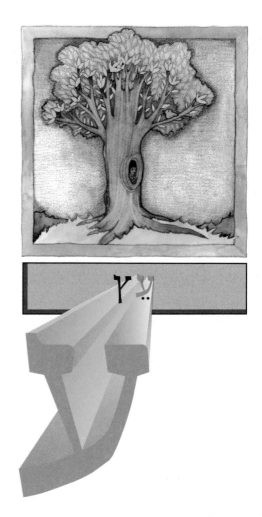

NAME THE LETTER

Circle the Hebrew letter named in the box.

מ	שׁ	(א)	ל	**ALEF**	1
ד	כ	ר	ו	**VAV**	2
צ	א	ק	ע	**TSADEE**	3
ר	ת	ב	ע	**DALET**	4
א	כ	ע	מ	**AYIN**	5
ע	ה	א	ק	**KOOF**	6

TWINS

Read aloud the sounds on each line.

Two sounds on each line are the same. Put a box around each of them.

On which line can you find עַ ?

_____

On which line can you find צַ ?

_____

Circle the letter with the sound "ts".

צָ   צַ

51

ע ע ע ע ע ע ע

COLOR THE SOUNDS

Read aloud the two Hebrew sounds in each balloon. Color the balloon if the two sounds are the same.

How many balloons did you color? _____

NUN

Color the Nun

SEARCH AND CIRCLE

Read aloud the sound each letter makes.

One letter on each line makes a different sound. Circle it.

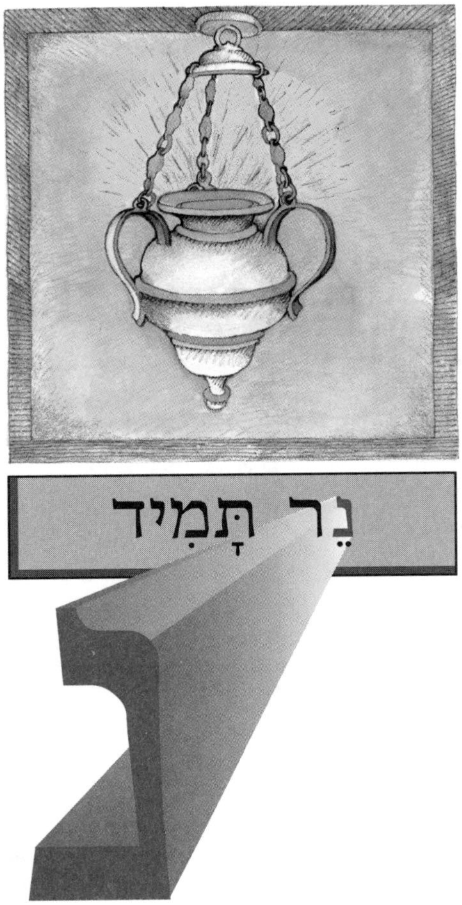

נֵר תָּמִיד

נ	(ת)	נ	נ	נ	1
נ	ד	נ	נ	נ	2
ו	נ	נ	נ	נ	3
כ	נ	נ	נ	נ	4
נ	נ	ב	נ	נ	5

53

SOUND MATCH

Read aloud the Hebrew sounds on each line.

Circle the Hebrew that sounds the same as the English in the box.

CHAH	1
NEE	2
VAH	3
KEE	4
EE	5
TSAH	6

DISCOVER THE LETTER

Color each space that has a dot to see the hidden letters.

Say the name and sound of the letters.

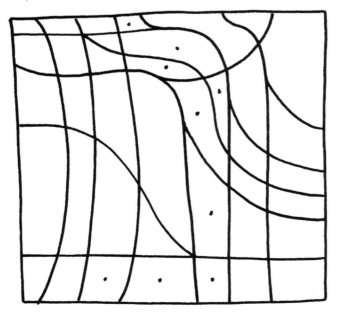
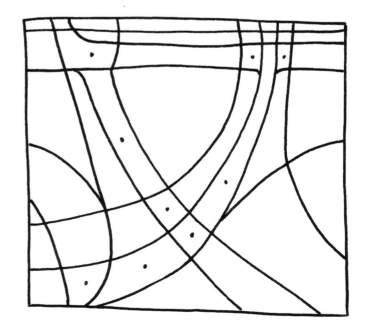

54

TRACE THE LETTER

נ   נ   נ   נ   נ   נ   נ

WHAT'S MISSING?

Circle the letter to complete the pattern in each row. Read aloud the sounds in each row.

ת	(ו)	ר		___	ה	ה	ד	ו	ה	ד	**1**
א	ע	ק		___	א	ל	ק	א	ל	ל	**2**
צ	ה	ד		___	ת	ר	צ	ת	ר	ר	**3**
שׁ	ע	ל		___	מ	שׁ	ע	מ	שׁ	שׁ	**4**
כ	ב	נ		___	ב	כ	נ	ב	כ	כ	**5**

TIC-TAC-TOE

Play tic-tac-toe with a friend. Read the sounds correctly to make an **X** or an **O**.

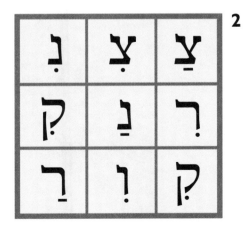

2

נֵ	צָ	צֶ
קֶ	נֶ	רִ
רֶ	וִ	קֶ

1

כְ	דָ	בֶ
כִ	בֶ	כֶ
בָ	כָ	דִ

Color the Ḥet

HET

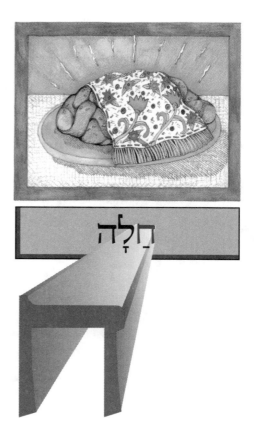

חָלָה

SEARCH AND CIRCLE

Read aloud the sound each letter makes.

One letter on each line makes a different sound. Circle it.

1

2

3

4

5

CONNECTIONS

Connect the Hebrew letter to its name. What sound does the letter make?

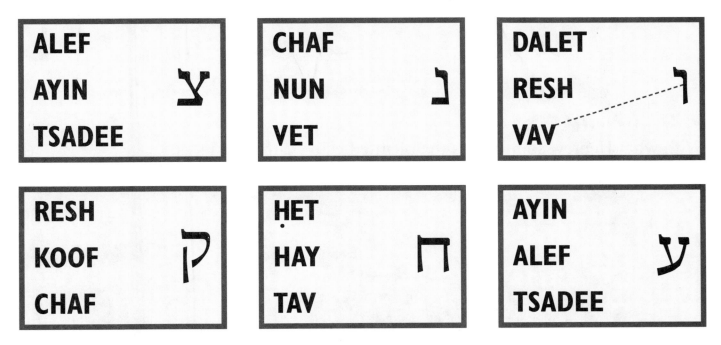

ALEF AYIN TSADEE	CHAF NUN VET	DALET RESH VAV
RESH KOOF CHAF	ḤET HAY TAV	AYIN ALEF TSADEE

SOUNDS LIKE

Read aloud the sounds on each line.

Circle the sounds that are the same.

TRACE THE LETTER

PICTURE MATCH

With what Hebrew sound does the picture begin? Circle the letter.

3	2	1
ת צ ח	ע ה ב	ב ד (כ)

6	5	4
ו נ שׁ	כ ר מ	א ק ל

58